WORLD DISASTERS!

DROUGHT

BRIAN KNAPP

STECK-VAUGHN
LIBRARY
Austin, Texas

Published in the United States in 1990
by Steck-Vaughn Co., Austin, Texas,
a subsidiary of National Education Corporation.
© Earthscape Editions 1989
© Macmillan Publishers Limited 1989

First published in 1989
by Macmillan Children's Books
A division of Macmillan Publishers Ltd

Designed and produced by Earthscape Editions,
Sonning Common, Oxon, England

Cover design by Julian Holland

Illustrations by
Duncan McCrae and Tim Smith

Printed and bound in the United States

1 2 3 4 5 6 7 8 9 0 LB 94 93 92 91 90

Library of Congress Cataloging-in-Publication Data

Knapp, Brian J.
  Drought.

  (World disasters!)
  "First published in 1989 by Macmillan Children's Books"—
T.p. verso.
  Summary: Examines the causes and effects of droughts and ways to prevent future disasters involving drought, particularly in the developing countries of the world.
ISBN 0-8114-2376-X
  1. Droughts—Juvenile literature. [1. Droughts]
I. McCrae, Duncan, ill.   II. Smith, Tim, ill.
III. Title.   IV. Series: Knapp, Brian J. World disasters!.
  QC929.D8K63   1990   363.3′492   89-19730

Acknowledgments

The publishers wish to thank OXFAM for their invaluable assistance in the preparation of this book.

Photographic credits

t = top b = bottom l = left r = right

All photographs are from the Earthscape Editions photographic library except for the following: 11, 32b Colorific; 9 NASA; 33b, 44tl M. Goldwater/Network; 33t, 34 OXFAM; 44-45 P. Walker/OXFAM; 28t J. Hartley/OXFAM; 31t, 35t, 43 M. Edwards/Panos Pictures; 16tl South West Water; 15, 7 Thames Water; 32t, 35b, 45br UNICEF.

Cover: Jim Richardson/WEST LIGHT
A dust storm blows across a Colorado farm.

Note to the reader
In this book there are some words in the text that are printed in **bold** type. This shows that the word is listed in the glossary on page 46. The glossary gives a brief explanation of words that may be new to you.

Contents

Introduction

A **drought** does not come suddenly like a storm or a flood. Nevertheless, it is no less a **disaster**. When **reservoirs** start to dry up, crops fail, animals and people suffer and perhaps die—that is a drought disaster. In many ways a drought is the worst of all disasters because the suffering it produces can last for months and sometimes even years.

One of the biggest areas of the world that suffers from drought is in Africa. It is called the **Sahel**, and in this region many of the world's worst drought disasters happen today. The drought-prone state of Rajasthan in northwest India is also a region of major disasters. Here a very large population depends on an area very much smaller than the Sahel.

Both the Sahel and Rajasthan are in an area just north of the **equator** where seasons are divided into those with rain and those that are dry. The plains here are covered with a mixture of small trees and grasses and called **savanna**. How much rain falls

◄ *There is nothing for these farm laborers to do. Without the rains the ground remains rock hard and cannot even be plowed.*

▼ *In many countries the most dramatic sign of a drought is an empty reservoir. The size of this reservoir can be seen by comparing it with the speedboat moving in the remaining water. About 90 percent of the water has been used to cope with a drought.*

depends on how far the moisture-bearing air from the equator reaches in the rainy season. Each year is different. As a result the rainfall is very unreliable. That is the reason why these areas of the world are most likely to have a drought.

In the parts of these areas that are farthest away from the equator, the rainfall dwindles to tiny amounts, and rain may not fall for several years. This pattern of weather produces a **desert**. There are no drought disasters in deserts because rain is not expected to fall there, and people get their water from special springs or wells, that bring water from deep underground.

The meaning of drought

Simply measuring drought in terms of the number of days without rain does not mean very much. How drought affects people is the important concern, and this varies from area to area.

▼ *Surviving a drought often means using up the food supply from the previous year's harvest. These farmers are letting the wind carry the dry skins from their stored onion crop. When these are used there will be no more.*

▼ *This boy is making an extraordinary journey because of a drought. His village has dug a shaft into limestone rock and then built steps so that they can reach water more than 160 feet underground. Each day he must make several journeys to fill the 5 gallon cans that are balanced on the pole over his shoulder.*

People adapt to the amount of water they know they can rely on. For example, in regions that receive rain regularly throughout the year (such as the northeast United States and Western Europe) there is usually no need to store much water. Few large reservoirs have been built because it is unlikely that these places will have a long dry spell. This means that, on the rare occasions when there has been no heavy rain for about 10 to 12 weeks, these small reservoirs start to empty. At this point a drought is declared and water officials attempt to cut down water use.

By contrast, many parts of the world have a dry period lasting several months each year. This is a normal part of the **climate** and people can adapt to it, as we shall see later. A drought in these places only occurs when there is too little rain in the wet season to allow crops to grow and reservoirs to refill.

Clearly, different parts of the world experience very different types of drought. To understand why this is so, we must learn a little about the way the **atmosphere** works.

▶ *These are fine weather clouds. When they occur in widespread shallow shapes as in this photograph, they will not develop into the tall giants needed to produce rain.*

▼ *This map shows the main places where drought disasters have occurred. Compare the pattern with the diagram on the right hand page. Most drought regions occur near to where air sinks.*

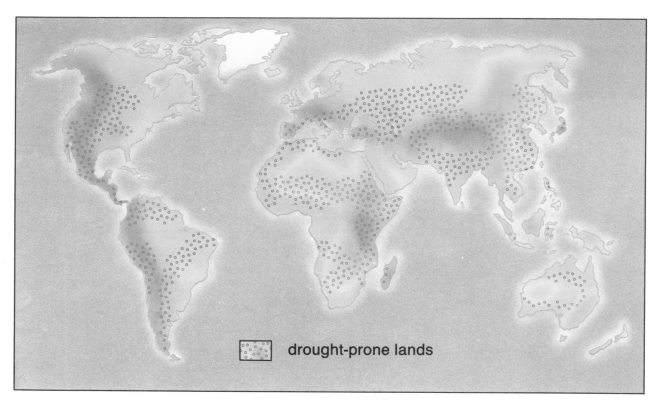

drought-prone lands

How the atmosphere works

The atmosphere is a huge blanket of gases covering the Earth. It has many layers, but only the lowest layer has weather. This layer, called the **troposphere**, is up to 25 miles thick and all the clouds form in it. Above lies the **stratosphere**, an air layer that acts like a lid, keeping all the weather firmly near the ground.

Air in the troposphere is constantly moving, driven by the heat from the sun. The sun shines down most fiercely on the **tropics** where the land gets very hot. In turn the land heats the air and causes it to rise. By contrast, the sun shines only weakly near the poles. The poles receive much less heat so that the land and the air are very cold and here the air sinks.

The contrast between the hot air at the tropics and the cold air near the poles causes the troposphere to churn over just like boiling water heated in a saucepan. This is called the circulation of the atmosphere. The flow of warm air to the Arctic and cold air back to the tropics helps to even out moisture across the Earth.

Clouds do not always mean rain

Rain starts in the world's great oceans. At the surface of the oceans water is continually being changed into a vapor and taken up in the air. This process is called **evaporation** and it makes the air moist. If the ocean is warm, it also shares its heat with the air, and the warm moist air starts to rise. Eventually, the moist air reaches the upper troposphere, where it cools. Here the moisture **condenses** into small droplets, forming the clouds we see. It is from these clouds that raindrops and snowflakes fall.

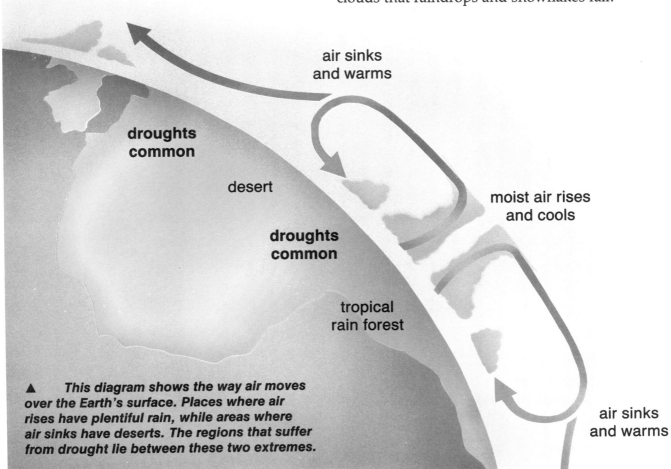

air sinks
and warms

droughts
common

desert

droughts
common

moist air rises
and cools

tropical
rain forest

air sinks
and warms

▲ *This diagram shows the way air moves over the Earth's surface. Places where air rises have plentiful rain, while areas where air sinks have deserts. The regions that suffer from drought lie between these two extremes.*

As rain or snow falls it has to pass through many thousands of feet of dry air. Evaporation occurs as the drops fall, so that all drops get smaller and smaller. In many cases the drop is completely evaporated before it reaches the ground. This is the reason why clouds do not always mean that it will rain. Places that have very dry air or very hot air will cause the most loss by evaporation. The world's deserts, for example, have the hottest and driest air on Earth.

Mountains that cause droughts

Evaporation of droplets is only one reason why there may be no rain. Sinking air is another reason. Just as condensation occurs and clouds form as air rises, so evaporation

takes place and clouds melt away as air sinks. Air that passes over a mountain range may be forced to rise as the wind reaches the side of the mountain. Here there will be large clouds and frequent rainfall. By contrast, when the air has passed over the mountain and reached the sheltered side, it will begin to sink. As air sinks, it warms and can absorb all the moisture once more. Droplets simply evaporate and the clouds melt away. The chances of rain on the sheltered side of a mountain are low. It is called the **rain shadow zone**. In extreme cases it causes a desert such as famous Death Valley in California. In other areas it simply makes drought more likely.

Regions where rain cannot reach

As the air circulates around the world, moisture and clouds can be carried many thousands of miles. Some clouds are carried from the oceans to the land where they release their moisture as rainfall. However, the farther the clouds travel from the oceans, the less likely they are to have enough moisture left for rain to fall.

▼   *This diagram shows the way air rises and falls over mountains in California, on its way east from the Pacific Ocean. Most rain falls on the mountains, but some falls in the valleys. Enough rain falls in the Owens Valley for crops to grow, but it often suffers from drought.*

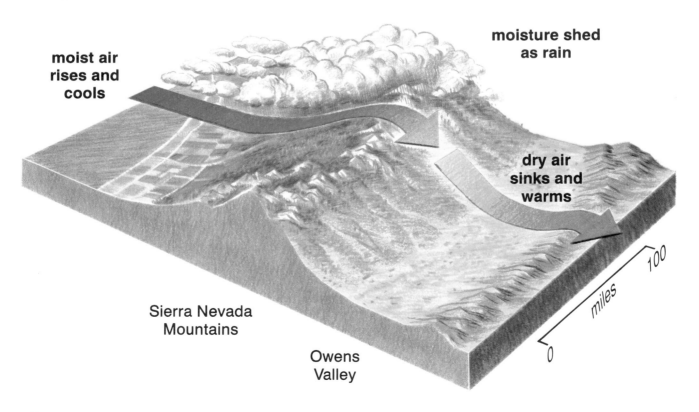

moist air rises and cools

moisture shed as rain

dry air sinks and warms

Sierra Nevada Mountains

Owens Valley

miles   100   0

This produces what we call **continental drought regions**. The "dust bowl" described on page 11, suffers from rain shadow and continental drought problems.

Where air spirals down

In the parts of the Earth that lie between the tropics and the polar regions, air is swirled around by the spin of the planet and it moves in broad spirals. In some spirals, called **depressions** or **lows**, the air rises and forms clouds. After each upward spiral there is a spiral that sends air back down to the surface. These are called **anticyclones** or **highs**. As air sinks in the high, it warms and stops clouds from forming.

Normally highs and lows travel around the Earth's midlatitudes as though on a conveyor belt. The highs are welcomed because they give a period of fine sunny weather. Sometimes, however, one of the highs remains stationary for a long time. These "blocking" highs steer all the lows carrying rain around them. Any region underneath a blocking high experiences a drought. This is what happened in Europe in 1976, as described on page 15.

▼ *This picture of the Earth from space shows the swirling regions of clouds called lows. It also shows highs. If highs last for too long in one place they will cause a drought.*

Drought

Drought has killed more people than any other disaster. Since droughts take a long time to set in, they don't make newspaper headlines until they are very severe.

Droughts have long-term effects. A drought may kill off crops and leave people without food. Then, in the following months, people die slowly of **starvation** unless they get help.

The Great American droughts

One of the world's most famous drought disasters happened in the American Great Plains in the early part of this century. The place where it occurred eventually became known worldwide as the "Dust Bowl." The story is one of inexperienced people using the land unwisely.

The United States is a young country. Its population grew swiftly as multitudes of immigrants arrived from Europe between 1850 and 1920. Much of the west then was still open range. As people moved into this open land, following famous routes such as the Santa Fe Trail, they knew little about the place they were going to. Settlers just started to farm where land seemed good.

The first disaster

Many early settlers arrived during droughts. They saw the short brown grass and the lack of rivers, and they called the area the "Great American Desert." They were not far wrong. It was a land that was to experience many a disaster.

The rainfall in the Great Plains changes from one year to the next. A few rainy years are often followed by a few dry years. The people who eventually settled on the plains arrived during some rainy years. They looked around and saw lush green grass, and couldn't understand why the earlier settlers had not stayed. There was no warning of drought.

These new settlers farmed in the way they had learned in Europe, and at first this was good. But then came the drought years and the people suffered. They had not kept much food aside for poor harvests. Their crops could not withstand the drought, which caused the crops to quickly wilt and die. Crops failed and people began to face hardship.

Then the winds began to blow. With no crops growing, there was nothing to hold the ground. The wind howled across the plains, **eroding** the precious topsoil and leaving the soil poor and unproductive. People looked on in despair and knew they would soon face hunger.

► **The Great Plains are wide flat lands. When a strong wind blows it can easily pick up soil from unprotected fields.**

Disaster hushed up

The state governments kept these disasters of the 1890s and 1910s as quiet as possible. They were still advertising for settlers to come to "this prosperous farmland."

The second of these disasters was suddenly replaced by a great demand for wheat from Europe where World War I had started. The price of wheat soared and huge new areas of fragile grasslands were put under the plow as people rushed to make a quick profit. Since the rainfall had improved, people thought everything was going to be all right.

The Dust Bowl

More disasters were in store. The worst one occurred in the 1930s. As the drought set in and the crops failed, the land was once more left open and unprotected. The bare soil blew away in the wind.

Drought was a big enough disaster by itself. But this was also the time called the **Great Depression**. Industries were in trouble and there was a lack of money even to buy food. Wheat prices were forced lower and lower. Banks would not lend farmers money to tide them over until the drought had ceased. Tens of thousands of farmers

◄ *During a dust storm the soil is blown into mounds, almost like sand dunes in a desert. Here you can see a farmer using his hat to help protect his face during a "blow." You cannot see the ground surface on this side of the fence because it is masked in a moving layer of soil. Notice how the soil is building up against the fence.*

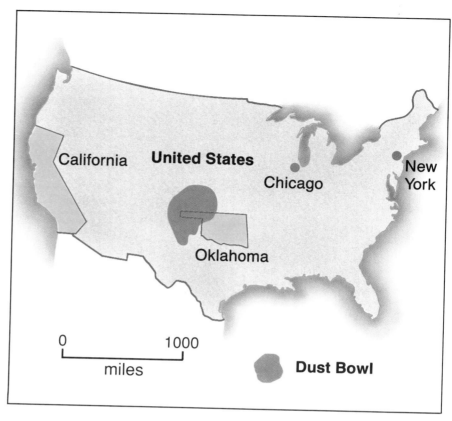

► *This map shows the Dust Bowl region of the United States in the 1930s.*

were forced off their land, ruined by low prices and low crop yields caused by the drought. The worst hit was Oklahoma. The penniless Oklahoma farmers who moved to California in search of new land came to be known as "Okies."

Emma's story

When the wind blew it started a dust storm blowing away the precious topsoil. Each dust storm took the farmers one step closer to disaster. A girl named Emma kept a diary of these terrible years. Emma was ten years old, and lived with her family in a wooden farmhouse on the Great Oklahoma Plains. From her bedroom window, she could see a line of telegraph poles going off into the distance, and she used them to work out how far she could see through the dust-laden air.

"This morning the wind blows as usual, slamming loose shutters against the walls time after time.

"I counted three poles today. That means I can see 140 yards. It's going to be a bad day. Yesterday I counted six poles because the wind was lighter. Papa went out to look at the wheat in our big field. When he came back he was almost in tears. He said the wind had rasped the soil across the wheat, wearing all the tops off like some giant file. He said if the wind blows for much longer there will be no crop this year.

"Today Papa is going to see if he can dig the tractor out. It is piled high all around with dust from the fields and it's half buried. He says if he can move it he'll take it into town and try to sell it. Mama needs the money real bad just to buy food to eat. She has been packing up our few belongings into bags. We don't have much because Mama has already pawned many of our clothes to get money for food.

"Mama and Papa agree that we must leave next week unless the weather gets better. They're hoping for the best, but the bank won't lend us more money for new seed, so I don't see how we can stay.

"Papa says there is good land out west in California and we'll do better there . . . I do hope he is right."

Eroded soil

This sad story of the "Dust Bowl" tells only part of the disaster. When rain came at last it fell in torrents, pounding the ground, and caking the surface hard. Instead of soaking in and giving moisture for plants to grow, the rain ran over the caked ground, carving great gullies in the bare soil. Rain was now the farmer's enemy too!

Repairing the damage

Drought and human foolishness combined had caused a disaster. Eventually the dust was blown right across the continent! It turned the clouds yellow as far north as Chicago and as far east as New York.

▼ *The Oklahoma landscape as it might have looked to Emma in the late 1930s.*

Only then did the government act, beginning a huge program of **soil conservation**. The government planted trees and grass in the gullies, they showed farmers how to keep moisture in the soil, and they developed new plants that could survive a drought. Over many years, slowly but surely, the land was made **fertile** again, and could be farmed once more. The price paid was very high.

Recent droughts

There have been other droughts in the "Dust Bowl," both in the 1950s and the 1970s, but neither has caused a disaster. This is because the government has helped farmers with money payments called **subsidies**. Nevertheless, the costs have been enormous. In some drought years the government has paid the farmers more money to treat their land carefully than the farmers made from selling their crops.

The Faucets Are Dry

Western Europe has one of the most reliable records of rainfall on Earth. Some places have rain so often that jokes are made about it. Yet the reliability of rain can also spell disaster where little trouble is taken to store water. The difficulty comes because Western Europe has such a high population that there are few places to store water, and the amount that has to be stored for so many people is very great.

▼ **This map shows the normal path of the jet stream, depressions, and anticyclones over Western Europe, and the changed pattern during the drought. The small map shows the percentage of the long term rainfall that fell during the drought.**

The reason for Europe's rain

The normally reliable rainfall is steered over Western Europe by a fast moving tube of air high in the troposphere. This is called the **jet stream**. Although it can't be seen, this tube of air is very powerful. It steers the weather across the midlatitudes with great wavy motions. Beneath one part of the jet stream lie the depressions. Here the jet stream sucks air from the ground and pulls cold air from the polar regions against warm air from the tropics. As the warm tropical air rides up over the cold, the air cools, clouds form, and rain is released. The air is lifted off the ground in a great spiral motion, and this is clearly picked out by the cloud pattern when seen from space.

Western Europe relies on this unseen jet stream to bring its rain as well as its fine weather. The jet stream does not, however, hold steady in one position. Instead it tends to twist around, sometimes arching into great

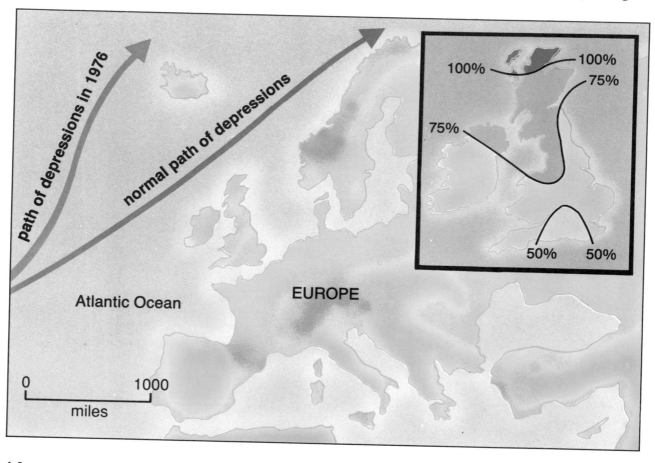

Path of depressions in 1976

normal path of depressions

100%   100%
        75%
75%
50%   50%

Atlantic Ocean

EUROPE

0   1000
    miles

loops, at other times almost straightening out. This unpredictable pattern causes each depression to be different from the one that went before. It is the reason why the weather in Western Europe is so unpredictable.

The Great Drought of 1976

In 1976 the jet stream pattern changed. It became fixed in one path, quite different from normal. The jet that brings the depressions with their rain often looped away across the Atlantic Ocean without skirting Western Europe, so the rain became irregular.

There were long periods of sunny weather as a high settled over Western Europe. At first everyone enjoyed the warmth of the sun. People enjoyed being able to sit in the warm air in their gardens and on the beach. It was the best summer anyone could remember. However, all the time the sun shone there was little rain. Weeks went by without enough rain to keep the plants from wilting. Slowly it dawned on everyone that such long periods of fine weather were not such a good thing after all. The land, the plants, and above all the reservoirs, were just not designed to cope with these unusual conditions.

The farmers' problems

Farmers were hit first. The winter of 1975 had also been very dry, with less than half the rainfall that was expected. As a result the soils did not fill up with water. There wasn't enough moisture in the ground for the plants to use in the warm weather of the spring when they grow fastest.

The farmers planted as usual, and the seeds began to sprout. But the jet stream kept most of the depressions away from Western Europe. As spring turned into summer, the rainfall was no better. The plants simply were not growing as fast as usual because the soil was dust dry.

The first plants to suffer a lot were those planted on chalk and sandy soils, where the water sinks through the soil and into the rock below. These soils dry out within weeks if there is no rain, and in 1976 they became like desert sand. Plants wilted and died before they even grew to full size. Soil started to blow away from the bare ground.

◀ ▲ *Tourists crowded the seaside resorts such as Brighton, England, in 1976, making the most of the sunshine. However, unseen in the countryside the reservoirs were drying up, as shown by the photograph on the left.*

The farmers on higher land fared little better. They rely on the rainwater to make grass grow and to feed the animals. But the rain did not come in sufficient quantities. The grass did not grow fast enough and soon the animals had stripped away what was there, leaving the ground bare. The hill farmers had to buy fodder from the lowland farmers at great expense. However, the drought had stopped the fodder crops from growing as well and there was little that could be offered. In desperation farmers began to buy fodder shipped in by boat from overseas. Meanwhile their fields turned brown as the drought set in further.

The faucets are dry

People in the cities saw little of the farmer's problems. They were protected from the early effects by water drawn from reservoirs. However, reservoirs only contain two percent of the normal flow of the rivers. If they are used without care, they will dry out within weeks. In the north of England cities like Leeds are supplied with water from a string of small reservoirs in the Pennine Hills. By mid-May 1976 the Leeds reservoirs were only half full. The

▼ *When water supplies to houses were turned off, people had to stand in line for water at street faucets.*

▼ *In many places crops would not grow because there was too little water. The remains had to be plowed into the dust dry soil.*

water officials started a "Save It" campaign to make the public realize how serious the problem was. Posters began to appear. The half-empty reservoirs were shown on television.

The public started to conserve and the reservoirs emptied less quickly, but the drought did not ease. By the middle of July the reservoirs were down to 42 percent of capacity, and they got lower every week. By the end of August they were below 30 percent. Soon, the water officials had to start imposing controls on water use. The drought had reached the cities.

By September the British government found there was a desperate situation. The country could not hold out much longer in many areas. The water mains had already been turned off and water tankers were being used to deliver small drinking supplies. Things became so bad the government appointed a "Minister for Drought." Luckily, no sooner had the "Minister" been appointed than the rain started. The drought was over and within weeks the "Minister for Drought" had to become the "Minister for Floods." Life in Europe was soon back to normal.

The use of hose pipes and sprinklers for domestic purposes is

BANNED

until further notice

Thames Water

◀ *This British poster was typical of many distributed by the water officials during the drought. Its purpose was to remind people that they couldn't use hoses and sprinklers during the emergency. It also served to remind people that they should be careful in the way water is used.*

Land Is Dust!

Drought strikes hardest at the poor. When drought struck the Great Plains in the 1930s, the people there were poor. Drought drove them from their land. In the 1970s the people of Britain were more prosperous. They withstood the drought by importing food. Today drought is a terrible problem for the **developing countries**.

Many developing countries are in places where rainfall is very unreliable. Much of the land bordering the great

Sahara Desert in Africa suffers greatly from drought and is often in the world news. Drought is also common in much of China and India. It isn't often reported in the world press because these two large countries have learned how to take care of themselves. Nevertheless, survival is at great cost as the recent drought in India shows. Astoundingly, 80 percent of the world's victims who are affected by natural disasters like droughts are Indians. In 1987 over 192 million people were affected by drought in India!

▼ *This map shows the normal pattern of the monsoon rains and the drought area.*

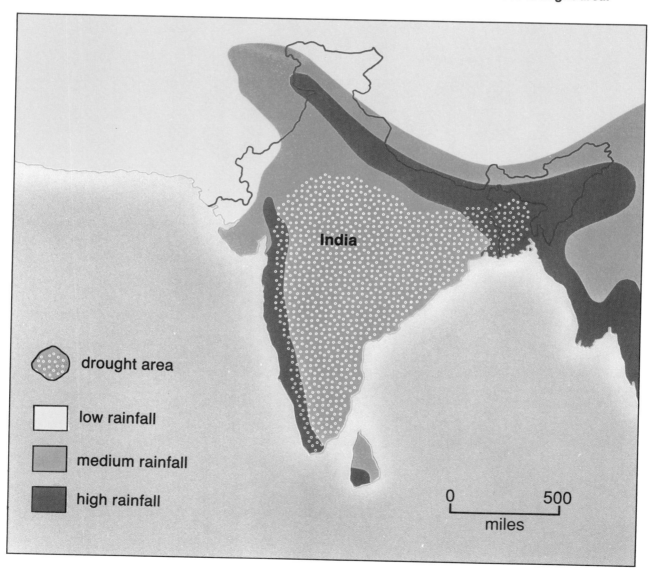

India

drought area

low rainfall

medium rainfall

high rainfall

0   500
miles

The drought sets in

India relies on the rain that falls in the season called the **monsoon**. This is the time, between June and September, when rain-bearing winds blow over the country from the Bay of Bengal and the Indian Ocean. Normally the start of the rainy season is very predictable. In each district the people know when the rains should arrive.

The monsoons are vitally important. They are the only chance the people have to grow the food needed to support over 700 million people. Some of the most fertile areas are in the north and northwest, and include the famous area called the Punjab. It is known as the "breadbasket of India," because much of the country's wheat is grown there.

In 1987 the rains were late in the Punjab and in many other states. As June moved to July the skies remained clear. Small puffy white clouds would appear but they would not grow. People were becoming desperate.

The days wore on. The tremendous heat that scorches the plains of India in early summer is normally cooled by the monsoon rains. This year the heat continued. Tempers frayed, partly because of the heat and partly because people were frustrated at not being able to get on with their farming. Some farmers stayed, determined to see the drought through. Many laborers were forced to leave because they could get no work on the farms. Here are the stories of two of these people.

▲ *In the scorching heat of the summer, women find shelter under umbrellas in the market of Jaipur, capital of stricken Rajasthan in India. In front of them are the piles of grain they are trying to sell.*

◀ *Rasoul and part of his family were determined to stay on the land.*

How people cope

By the first week in August, Rasoul Pal had watched five weeks of the monsoon season go by without rain. He began to lose hope for the seeds he had planted on his tiny fields. He was increasingly fearful of the outcome. He knew that the season would be a failure. There would be no harvest for his family and no food for his cattle. "This year the cattle will surely starve," he thought. Huts had been stripped of their thatched roofs to provide fodder for the animals in the hope that better days would return. However, so far there were no signs of this.

Rasoul had about one and a quarter acres of land, little enough to survive on even in a good season. It took all his energy just to keep this much land hoed and weeded. During the weeks of drought Rasoul continued to hoe the dusty soil. He had no access to water and all he could do was wait for the rains. The seeds that were sown sprouted only in patches and none grew to more than withered seedlings.

Rasoul had other worries. Where could he find money to buy food for his family? He had to find food for 12 mouths. In the market, the little grain that was available was being sold at very high prices. Rasoul also had to pay for the fertilizer he sprinkled on the ground with the seeds. He had borrowed the money for this through a bank—would the bank be understanding?

Why people leave the land

Ashish's story was different. He decided to leave the land. He, like many others, had been made jobless by the drought which had destroyed the crops. So he decided to move to another district where he hoped to get a job under the food-for-work program set up by the government.

He and his family gathered a string bed, pots, and some other essentials, and loaded them on their remaining buffalo. Ashish, his shrunken, emaciated face almost hidden beneath his hat, held his smallest son with one hand while he gently prodded the buffalo with the other. His wife carried a baby in her arms. They moved silently, unmindful of the traffic, trudging along the road to an unknown destination.

▲ *Ashish was resigned to leaving the land.*

▶ *Although the sky is cloudy, no rain fell during the 1987 drought. As a result the rivers remained dry.*

The side effects

Drought is unlike other forms of natural disaster. It does not strike quickly or end quickly. Drought goes on and on. Eventually, hunger can drive people to desperation. Food riots are a natural consequence of starvation. Disease is a natural partner to hunger. With wells running dry, many people are forced to drink tainted water, so **epidemics** break out.

Determined to survive

Despite all the hardships, people are still determined to see a drought through if they possibly can. In August a senior Indian government official announced that there had been the lowest rainfall this century.

"The year 1987 has been the worst monsoon of the century. Rainfall has been either deficient or scanty in two-thirds of the country. We are in deep trouble." He then thought for a moment and added, "But we will overcome the crisis."

▲ *When drought strikes and people are forced to leave the land, they must take up whatever work they can find. This young woman is breaking stones in a quarry. It is hard and dangerous work.*

◄ *This slum in the middle of India's capital, Delhi, is the final destination of many people who leave the land. The Indian government works hard to find ways of helping people in the countryside because it doesn't want the slums to grow any larger.*

How Nature Copes

Drought takes effect slowly and may last for months or years. The natural world has developed many ways of dealing with this problem. To understand how this works it is first useful to know something about the way water moves through the ground.

Water in the ground

When rain falls, some of it runs straight to rivers and flows to the sea. Much more falls on plants. In a storm, the water soon begins to drip from plant leaves and onto the soil.

The soil is the first line of protection against drought. Water flows into the soil through gaps called **pores**. The pores are very small so some water is trapped and held for future use. In many ways the soil is like a giant sponge. When all the soil pores are full, surplus rainwater pushes its way down to the rock below.

The rock is the second line of defense against drought. Some rocks, such as limestone, chalk, and sandstone, have small pores and cracks within them. Rocks which allow water to move through them are called **aquifers**. Rock layers are much thicker than the soil, therefore the layers can store much larger quantities of water.

Water flows out of the soil through stream banks, and it sometimes flows out of the rock as **springs**. Elsewhere it flows out into the riverbed and remains unseen. In general water flows more slowly through rock than soil, but both sources keep the streams flowing when there is no rainfall. It is the slow release of water from soil and rock that prevents a drought for many weeks without rain.

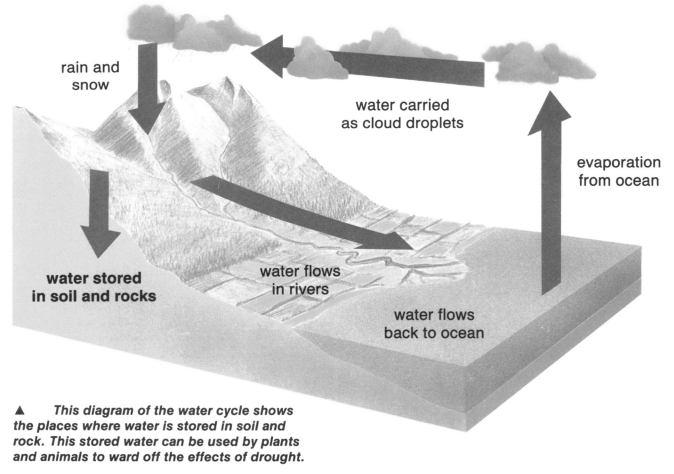

▲   *This diagram of the water cycle shows the places where water is stored in soil and rock. This stored water can be used by plants and animals to ward off the effects of drought.*

▲ *This is an evergreen Joshua tree. Its needlelike leaves are very waxy and do not lose water easily.*

Planning to survive

Both plants and animals need water for survival. However, both have to adopt very different means if they are to survive a drought. Plants have to make do with the water trapped in the soil. The soil becomes dry long before streams cease to flow, so plants have to have special ways of slowing down their water needs quickly. They must also be good at getting the last drop of moisture from the soil. Animals can travel to streams and water holes to find the water they want. In a drought most animals run out of food to eat before their sources of water dry up.

Water for plants

Plants use water that has been stored in soil pores. In dry areas plants naturally tend to grow some distance apart, giving each of them a chance to tap water from a large area when there is no rain.

Plants that grow naturally in areas with a drought have two ways of coping with dry soil. Many plants have long roots that sink deep into the soil and sometimes

◄ *The spiky drought-resistant plant in this picture looks as though it is dead. However, it simply has very small leaves so that it does not lose water too quickly. The cacti in the picture store water inside their bulblike stems.*

into the aquifer below. Other plants spread out huge nets of roots through the soil and thus gather moisture from a wide area.

Plants also have ways of stopping water evaporating from their leaves. In areas with a regular dry season many plants shed their leaves (they are **deciduous).** When the dry period is less predictable plants have to keep their leaves so that they can grow quickly when the rain comes. Instead they often have thick and waxy leaves, with very few pores through which they can lose water.

The way plants grow

Plants that grow naturally on dry soils have traded survival for growth. They will not perish in a drought, but they will not grow fast either. They do not normally make very attractive **food crops** for people.

The most productive food crops, like rice, will not survive without continual supplies of water. If people want to grow these crops they will have to provide a continual supply of water, a technique called **irrigation**. Otherwise they will have to be content to grow crops, like millet, that will survive. It is a hard and costly choice.

Animals and drought

There are many animals that can withstand drought. Some types of deer never need to drink at all. They get all the moisture they need through the leaves that they eat. Other

---

▼   *This magnificent baobab tree uses its giant trunk to store water. It is deciduous, shedding its leaves when water is scarce. Many animals, and especially elephants, will eat the trunk of the baobab during a drought to get at the moisture.*

animals have special sacs for storing water. The camel can drink up to 12 gallons of water at a time. After it drinks all this water a camel looks swollen. This water will allow a camel to go for several days without drinking at all. This is a vital benefit in areas where drought may have reduced drinking water to a few scattered **water holes**. Camels will need to **browse** far and wide in order to find enough food and they cannot keep returning for water.

In a drought it is important to **conserve water**. This is most easily done by keeping out of the direct heat of the sun or away from drying winds. Many animals stay cool and conserve water by coming out to look for food only at night.

▶ *Goats are highly adaptable animals. They will eat any sort of vegetation to get to food during a drought. The thorny branches of the tree shown in this picture have not put off the goats. They have climbed the trunk and are eating among the branches.*

◀ *The camel is the animal best known for surviving long periods without water. These animals have recently been to a water hole and are still swollen. Notice how little vegetation there is in the area. In such places animals will only survive if they search widely for all the small plants still growing.*

25

Why People Die

The world's pattern of weather naturally makes life harder in some places. As a result there are certain danger areas where people are more likely to suffer from drought. Together the drought-prone lands make up 30 percent of the land area of the globe and affect about 600 million people. This makes drought an important worldwide problem.

Each continent has its own danger areas. In Africa they lie between the parched lands of the true deserts and the lush regions of the rain forests. This region is the Sahel. In India the parched lands lie to the north and east, around Delhi. In central Asia there are large dry areas that stretch across China to central Russia. In North America the drought areas are in the southwest, and the Great Plains, while in South America they lie in Argentina and Chile. In Australia, the entire central and western regions are drought prone. These areas are shown on the map on page 6.

◄ *In a wealthy country such as the United States, the problem of drought can be overcome by storing water in reservoirs. This picture shows the Hoover Dam and part of Lake Mead, which borders Arizona and Nevada.*

► *In a poor country there may not be enough money to build many reservoirs and people will have to take care of their own needs. This man is digging for water in a river-bed. It took him 15 minutes to find enough water to fill the container.*

Rich and poor countries

In the drought areas, each year is different and the rainfall is very unreliable. Drought has caused the biggest disasters the world has ever known. However, the death toll has not been evenly spread. Whether or not many people die depends on the wealth of a country.

A wealthy country can spend money sinking wells and pumping water from aquifers deep underground. It can spend money importing food from abroad until the crisis is over. A wealthy country will continue to sell goods from stores and there will be no real shortages. Only a small number of people farm the land. Few livelihoods are at stake.

A poor country, on the other hand, has little money for wells and pumps, and it cannot afford to import food from abroad. In a poor country distribution of food is always difficult because there are few roads.

Many people are scattered across the countryside, so it is difficult for them to walk to the markets. Reaching shops may involve days of walking. Above all, a poor country has large numbers of people making a living from the land, so that a great many lives are at stake.

People who suffer most

If a drought affects a poor country there is little cash available to help. As the drought sets in the number of people who need help may become too large for the government to handle. The amount of food distributed per person gets smaller and smaller. In the end the long period on low rations makes

▼   *This map shows where the main drought-prone lands lie. It also shows such lands in wealthy countries. As you can see, many of the drought-prone lands are not in wealthy countries. When disaster strikes, they will need aid from the wealthier nations.*

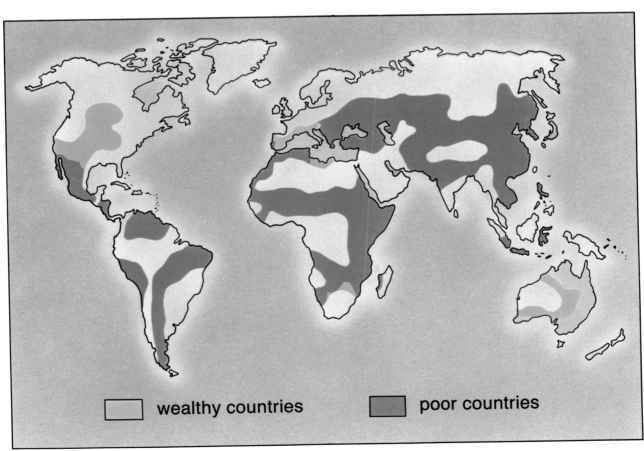

wealthy countries   poor countries

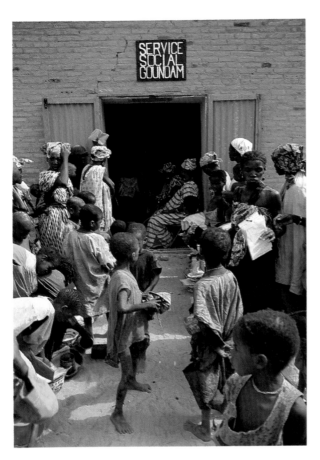

people weak and more likely to get sick. Many people do not die directly from starvation, they die from diseases brought on by **malnutrition**.

The people who get most food are those in the towns, because they are the easiest to reach if transportation is bad. People in the countryside do less well, since on their scattered farms they are much harder to reach. Their crops are ruined by the drought and they have little money to buy food. These are the people who suffer most. In the end their only hope will be to move to the cities or relief camps set up by the government or overseas **aid agencies**.

◄ *People wait patiently for food aid at a local distribution center.*

▼ *This woman kneels on the ground, picking up every last grain of corn that has been dropped from bags during a distribution of food. She knows that every grain is vital to the survival of her family.*

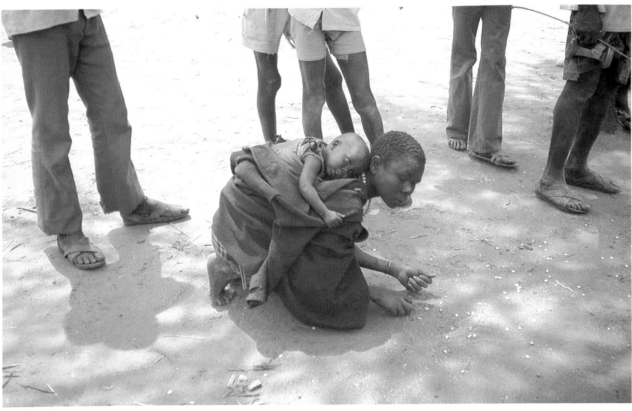

People help to make droughts

A drought may not be entirely due to lack of rain. Droughts can be made worse by the way people overwork the land. A combination of overworked land, low rainfall, and rapidly increasing numbers of people, brings on disaster and death.

In many areas people have learned how to cope with drought over many generations. They are not ignorant of the causes of their disaster, but they find themselves trapped. Their populations are rising and they have to use the land more and more intensively. There is no money for fertilizer so the land soon yields less when overworked. To try to get more yield the farmers work the land even harder.

In this vicious circle enough rain is crucial just to survive. A drought that might have given people a hard time in years past becomes a disaster today when there are so many more mouths to feed.

▲　*If the land is bare when the rains come, the torrential downpours will beat the topsoil into a hard crust. Further rain cannot soak into the soil and plants cannot get enough water to grow. This is a common feature in much of Africa.*

◄　*In a drought both people and animals suffer. If the animals die from lack of food, the people will have nothing, and they are then also in danger of starvation.*

Great Disasters

Drought kills people—slowly. When a drought kills off crops, it leaves people without food. Then people begin to die of starvation. This is what happened in all the droughts shown in the table on the next page. Notice how many people have died, even in this century.

▼ **This chart shows the way rainfall has declined in the Sahel countries south of the Sahara Desert during recent decades. The disaster in the late 1960s and early 1970s occurred because the gradual decline in rainfall had made crop yields low in the years before the main drought set in. The people had little stored away to see them through such a bad period.**

Why disasters happened

The world's greatest droughts have occurred mainly in Asia. Large areas of this continent have only irregular rainfall. In these areas farms are often small and use few modern methods of production. As a result, farmers are only able to meet the needs of their families in a good rainfall year. When droughts come there is little stored food to carry people over the crisis. In these areas transportation has also been poor, making it impossible to get food from areas of plenty into the places of need.

In recent years there has been much progress in building up food stocks in Russia, India, and China. It is unlikely that deaths on such a large scale will ever happen there again. Transportation networks have been improved and help should be available. In the years ahead Africa will be the problem area and tragedies here may add to the long death list.

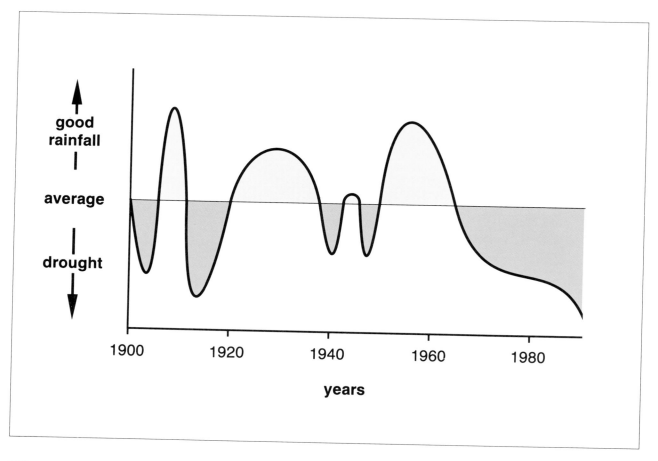

years

In the past the scale of a drought disaster has been measured by the numbers who have died. Although it is unlikely that people will die in such large numbers in the future, disasters will still happen. The size of a drought stricken area is often so huge that the number of people that suffer is also immense. This is what makes a drought so difficult to overcome. Finding food for five million people, for example, may be impossible because the world reserves are just not that great!

◀ *This picture tells of a great disaster. Animals and people are forced to drink water from the same tank. All the land around has been laid to waste by overgrazing and wind erosion.*

Estimated Deaths from Droughts

Year	Country	Number of Deaths
1333–37	China	over 4 million
1769–70	India	between 3 and 10 million
1837–38	India	800,000
1865–66	India	10 million
1876–78	India	3.5 million
1876–79	China	between 9 and 13 million
1891–92	Russia	400,000
1892–94	China	1 million
1896–97	India	5 million
1899–1900	India	1 million
1920–21	China	500,000
1921–22	Russia	5 million
1932–33	Russia	5 million

Emergency

Drought disasters come in many forms. In **developed countries** they may be so severe that industry has to close down to conserve water. This can put the jobs of many people at risk. In both the developed countries and developing countries drought also hits crops hard. A drought disaster can bring ruin to many farmers, but may also bring starvation to whole nations.

In the future drought disaster is most likely in the developing countries. Some countries have already found ways to cope with the problem while others must still keep fighting. Here we will look at what steps can be taken in an emergency in the developing world.

▶ *In an emergency developing world people often have to rely on outside help. Here you see American flour being unloaded at the docks in Ethiopia.*

▶ *A drought emergency in a developed country usually means no more than the need to stand in line at a water tanker.*

The onset of drought

Droughts become disasters slowly. The period with little or no rain stretches from weeks to months, and there is time to plan for food distribution. No one should be taken by surprise. Governments have problems when they do not watch the situation.

Sometimes the lack of water becomes critical quickly. This happens in countries that have only one wet season a year. These countries must have enough rain for their crops to grow and they have no second chance of planting. The farmers do not know whether the rains will come until the last time for planting is reached. Countries like India, Ethiopia, Sudan, and Somalia can find a drought disaster bearing down on them within a few weeks.

◄ *The result of drought is frequently too little food. This often shows most dramatically in the thin, helpless bodies of children. This child was too weak to eat solid food and had to be given liquid food for his recovery.*

◄ *A drought often causes many people to leave their homes in search of food for their families. These people have been walking for weeks toward an emergency supply camp in Sudan.*

The first steps

Here is an extract from a telex dated August 19, 1987. The message was sent by the field director of the aid agency OXFAM to their Oxford, England headquarters. It shows the massive scale of an emergency that had to be dealt with.

"TWO THIRDS OF INDIA IS AFFECTED . . . IN WORST AFFECTED AREAS RAINFALL HAS BEEN LESS THAN 60% OF NORMAL . . . PRESENT DROUGHT IS SAID TO BE THE WORST THIS CENTURY . . . CROPS SOWN WHERE SOME INITIAL RAIN NOW COMPLETELY DESTROYED, AND AT LEAST 15 MILLION LANDLESS AND MARGINAL FARMERS WITHOUT WORK . . ."

Good management in previous years meant that the government was able to meet this emergency. This is how they did it:

In the 1950s and 1960s India began to use new farming methods. Because the new methods were so much more successful at producing food than the old methods the new system was called the **Green Revolution**. The Green Revolution has given India extra food in most years. Some was stockpiled for an emergency such as a drought. In the 1987 emergency Prime Minister Rajiv Gandhi was able to use part of the stockpile to prevent people from starving when the crops in their fields shriveled and died. The food was taken from storehouses and distributed by train to all the stricken areas. Thus the first steps were to prevent a drought disaster from becoming a famine.

Although the government has been able to prevent starvation, the price has been high. The huge and unending scale of the drought has cost the government much of its carefully saved stockpile.

The next steps

During an emergency the government must do more than just supply food. A drought emergency may last for months. Many people who worked on the land as laborers will be without jobs, and will start to move to the cities in search of work. This would put a heavy strain on the cities. The government's job is to provide food in the countryside and also to provide some form of work. This can be done cheaply by a food for work program.

▶ *Children often need different food than adults. Here an emergency aid team is giving special food to children. Notice one of the workers is keeping records. This is to make sure all the children get an adequate diet.*

Programs to give food for work deal with the emergency in two ways. Governments provide food that is not charity, allowing people to keep their self-respect; and they get drought prevention programs under way cheaply. People work at digging new **wells** for drinking water, and digging existing wells deeper so that they can withstand a severe drought without running dry. People are employed in digging **terraces** to stop future rains from eroding the soil. Workers build dams in rivers to help water sink into the riverbed, and reservoirs to provide irrigation water in the future. People can also see that their efforts are doing them good, and this helps to keep up their spirits.

Looking after animals

A drought affects people, their crops, and animals. Drought means that the fodder to feed animals cannot be grown. Without water and fodder, the animals will die. It will be a tragedy for the animals and also for the people who rely on them for meat, milk, and to pull plows. During the emergency it is important to find food for the animals if possible, because a country without animals will find it harder to cultivate enough land after the drought.

▲　*During an emergency people can be asked to work for the food they are given. These men are being given their food after working all day in the fields. They have been digging terraces which will help guard against soil loss in the future.*

◄　*In an emergency animals need to be given water. In areas where it is possible, the digging of many new wells would help to relieve the pressure on existing wells and would allow animals to seek food over larger areas.*

Be Prepared

Drought affects the world's people in many different ways. In countries such as the United Kingdom, little rainfall for a few weeks can bring reserves to a low level. This is because some people are not used to worrying about how much water they use. Water is not metered in the same way as electricity, and it might not make much difference to some people's financial situation if they waste it. On average the water used is over 40 gallons per head per day.

In countries such as Kenya, where people have to be careful how each last drop is used, the way developed countries use water must seem wasteful. In areas where there is a long dry season people use water very carefully. Many people can make do with less than 2.5 gallons per head per day. A drought here means a whole year when there is not enough rain for crops to grow.

▲ *This woman is helping to explain to her fellow farmers new ways of conserving water.*

► *Preparing for a drought can be done within the community. Here a group of villagers are making a small earth dam which will hold back rainwater.*

Different plans

How a drought is prepared for depends on the country involved. A developed country with high technology, for example, would not use the same plan as a farming country with low income. A country that expects a drought to last only a few weeks would not adopt the same plan as a country where drought might last for years. Some plans would also use expensive energy in the form of fuel to pump water from one place to another. More modest plans would expect people to get their own water, or to use natural slopes to move water to where it is needed.

There are only three options for people preparing to survive a drought. Water can be stored in times of plenty for times of need; less water can be used to make the natural supply last longer; and people can move away to a place where rain is more plentiful. All three plans are used by people in different countries.

Dams and reservoirs

People's lives are least disturbed if water can be stored against a drought. When it is needed the water is simply released and most people will not even realize that a drought has occurred.

This kind of preparation costs a lot of money. Most industrial countries have chosen it as the way forward. Some developing countries who could raise the money have also used this system.

Large dams are built in upland areas where there is plentiful rainfall. The dams are placed across rivers creating large reservoirs. The rivers chosen are usually those that also run through places that might suffer drought. When a drought sets in, water is released from the reservoirs into the rivers. By allowing plenty of water to flow down the rivers, areas with drought problems are able to take water from the rivers when necessary.

▼ *This large dam near Boise, Idaho, has a clear message to the public painted on it. Drought can make forests tinder dry. If forests catch fire, forest loss will be added to loss of crops and the toll from drought will be even greater. People can reduce the risk by being careful.*

Some of the biggest dams and reservoirs in the world have been built to prevent drought problems. The Hoover Dam (shown on page 26) and the Glen Canyon Dam on the Colorado River in Arizona, hold back the snowmelt waters of the Colorado. This water is taken to the big city centers of California by means of open channels called **aqueducts**. The Elephant Butte Dam on the Rio Grande in Texas allows water to be taken all through the year for irrigation of the nearby fields. In central Wales, the Clywedog and the Elan Valley reservoirs store water for the industrial Midlands of England.

Some of the biggest dams are in the developing world. There is a whole network of dams in Pakistan to control the flow of the Indus River. In Egypt the Nile River no longer flows straight to the sea because its waters have been trapped behind the Aswan High Dam to make Lake Nasser. The whole Nile Delta region is watered from this one reservoir 125 miles long. In Nigeria the Kainji reservoir traps the Niger waters, and in Ghana the Volta River has been trapped to make one of the world's largest lakes.

Diverting water

It is not always possible to find rivers that can be dammed to make reservoirs and also flow into areas of need. In these cases an expensive way of guarding against drought is to divert the water. This involves building a dam and reservoir on one river, then digging a tunnel through the hill or mountainside and carrying the water by pipe until it reaches the river where it is needed.

There are some very impressive plans that achieve diversion of water. In the United Kingdom, the water from one of Europe's largest reservoirs, the Kielder reservoir, is diverted in tunnels through the surrounding hills so that it can be taken to areas of need. Eventually the water flows into a river that supplies the industrial area of Teesside, over 50 miles to the south.

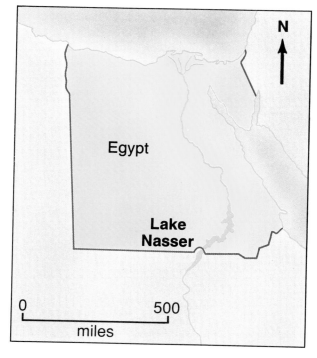

◄ ▲ *This photograph shows Lake Nasser in Egypt. It is held back by the Aswan High Dam. The land on either side of the lake is desert. The Egyptian government got financial help from the Soviet Union for this expensive project.*

Perhaps the most impressive plan of all is the water diversion across the Rocky Mountains. In this example the parched Great Plains receive water from the Colorado River. Water that would have flowed west to the Pacific Ocean is pumped up part of the Rockies, through a tunnel driven into a mountain summit, and then let down to the other side. From here it flows into the Platte River. The Platte is a tributary of the Mississippi River and its waters flow east to the Gulf of Mexico.

Using groundwater

In many parts of the world it is not necessary to build great dams and create large lakes. This is because many of the rocks beneath dry areas are aquifers. These water-bearing rocks can be tapped by sinking deep wells and pumping the water out.

The cost of doing this is high, but the water used goes directly to the fields or to the public drinking supply. London's water comes mostly from the chalk rock beneath

◄ *This picture shows circular fields in the Great Plains. At the center of each field is a well. Water is fed from the well into a long sprinkler arm that travels in a circle.*

▼ *Irrigation is the lifeblood of drought-prone lands. The area shown in this photograph lies in a rain shadow valley between mountains. It can only produce a reliable crop if irrigation is used all the time.*

the city; California's San Joaquin Valley waters its oranges and grapes with water pumped from the aquifer below; and there is no longer as large a "Dust Bowl" on the Great Plains because water is pumped from underground to irrigate the fields.

It is also possible to raise water from wells by hand, and this is done in many countries in the developing world for local use. It provides a good, clean, and reliable supply for drinking, but without pumps the amounts that can be raised are too small to water plants.

Conserving water in the soil

It is simply not possible to store all the water needed for a long drought. In many countries the biggest part of the plan is to help the soil to store as much water as possible. This is done by terracing the land so that the rainwater does not run away as soon as it has fallen, but sinks in instead.

Many terraces are dug by hand. It is a system that can be used by people even if they have little money, because it can be done on a small scale as well as on a big one. Today most countries have large parts of their steep cropland terraced, and more terraces are being built each year.

Storing household water

In many parts of the world people are out of reach of piped water and they have to store their own water against a drought. They do this in many ways, but one of the most popular is in stone jars. These are bulb-shaped concrete tanks that are fed by rainwater from the roof. Even a small jar can last a family for many weeks if they use the water carefully. A trench dug around the house can also feed water into a pit dug into the ground. If this pit is lined and covered it will hold enough water to provide for farm animals during a drought.

◄ *This dam is placed across the river to hold back water at the end of the rainy season. This encourages water to sink into the riverbed, where it is stored until needed during a drought.*

► *Small scale plans can be very effective. These villagers have built a wall around a natural rocky hollow to store a little more water to tide them over a long dry spell.*

Changing the style of living

Traditionally many people who experienced frequent drought became **nomads**. That is, they moved to where the rains were falling. Many tribes in Africa and Asia moved with the seasons. They did not have the machinery to build dams and so they followed nature. Unfortunately, with a much bigger population today, it is increasingly difficult to move at will because other people have settled on the nomadic lands. It is a way of preparing for drought that is no longer an option for the future.

Changing farming

Some countries depend very heavily on their farm produce. In these places, preparing for drought means concentrating on producing more crops in the wetter areas and fewer in drier areas. No amount of hard work in the field will save crops in the very dry areas (12-20 inches of rainfall a year) from total failure about every third year. To make the best use of the land governments should help these people raise livestock.

In regions with a little more rainfall (20-30 inches a year) the chances of failure are only 1 year in 5, and the yield per acre is three times that of the drier belt.

Timing is most important for successful farming in these areas. If crops grow well and ripen in a short time farmers can make use of even small amounts of rain. Plant breeders can often develop crops that match the period during the rainy season when the chances are highest that there will be enough rain. Improving the drought resistance of crops might also cut down the number of failures in such areas.

Preparing for drought also means looking at different farming areas at the same time. More crops should be planted in areas where the rains are good, and livestock should be farmed where rains are poor. If people in the two zones can trade with each other, both groups will benefit.

▼ *Collecting water from the roof in a stone jar provides each household with a convenient supply of water and saves much carrying.*

Waiting for Disaster

We have seen how people can try to change their lives to prevent disaster. Why don't they use this knowledge? Why do they remain in drought–prone areas?

These are difficult questions. Let's look at Ethiopia. It is a mostly mountainous country in northeast Africa with a population of just under 50 million—about the same as England. Ethiopia has one of the fastest growing populations in the world. It is also one of many countries in Africa that suffer from drought.

Ethiopia has been in the world headlines for many years and will probably remain there for many years to come. There is a dreadful combination of drought, growing population, and civil war. Those who suffer are the ordinary farmers, the people on whom the country still depends.

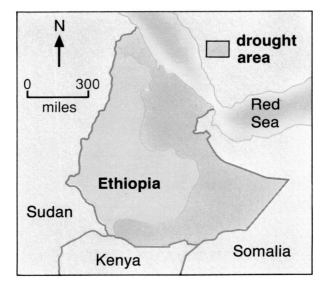

▲ *Ethiopia lies near the Sahara desert. Countries near deserts often suffer from drought.*

▼ *This picture of an Ethiopian village set among its fields, and with trees for shade, was taken before the ravages of drought forced people to make massive changes to the landscape.*

The need to farm

To understand why people do not move from drought stricken areas, you need to understand why they were there in the first place. Ethiopia was a naturally fertile region, with large areas suited to farming. It was called the "breadbasket of Africa."

For generations the Ethiopian people farmed their land without trouble. However, mountain soils are easily washed away during the wet season storms if left uncovered by vegetation. Farmers have always been aware of the problem of soil erosion, but in the past they were able to leave the land to rest and recover (lie **fallow**) every few years.

Recently this has changed. Increasing numbers of mouths to feed has meant that the farmers can no longer leave their tired soils fallow. Nowadays, when the rains come they beat down on bare land and wash the soil away, ton after ton. The Ethiopian highlands are losing about three billion tons of soil a year.

Erosion leaves the soil sandy, coarse, and infertile. In this condition it cannot hold as much water, so there is less for the plants to use for growth. The farmers of Ethiopia have paid the price for **overuse of land**. Drought comes sooner now simply because the soil cannot hold as much moisture as it used to.

Farmer's problems

It would be possible for the farmers to stop much of the erosion by building terraces. However, terraces require enormous amounts of hard work to build. Everything has to be done by hand, and it is a slow, painful task. At the moment farmers need all their time just to get the soil to yield enough for survival.

▼ *A combination of soil abuse and drought have caused much of the land in Ethiopia to become barren and wasted. Dust storms are now commonplace.*

▲ *This man's crop has only produced tiny ears of corn because of drought. They are not worth harvesting. His year's effort has gone to waste.*

Farming has made the land more liable to drought in other ways. Over 40 percent of Ethiopia was once covered with forest. Much of the forest has been cleared to get firewood, to allow more land to be plowed, and to give more pastures for the large herds of animals. Trees are well known to be helpful in preventing soil erosion. They can also help to retain moisture in the soil. As forests are cut back, the soils wash away faster and faster.

These examples show that improvements in farming have not kept up with the needs of a rising population in a difficult land. Overworking the soil has caused yields to fall as low as a fifth of traditional levels.

Resettlement

One way of helping would be to move families away from the north, which is overpopulated and very dry. These families could be resettled in the south which is still fertile and has fewer people. If this resettlement were successful, fewer people would be liable to suffer when the next drought comes and the crops on the overworked soils fail.

Why the drought hit so hard

In 1984 and 1985 there was a severe drought that affected the whole of Ethiopia. This was not the first drought to be felt there. The drought of 1972-1974, for example, had caused the deaths of 200,000 people. The new drought looked as though it would prove even more devastating.

Around ten million people were affected. The numbers of dead did not rise above 100,000 because, on this occasion, about 1.5 million tons of food was shipped in from overseas as aid.

The disaster was so bad because Ethiopia's agriculture could not make the best use of the small amounts of water. Furthermore, the government could not help sufficiently because of lack of money. There was not enough help to train farmers in the new ways. During the drought there were no trucks to move food or other aid effectively. Even when trucks came from abroad they could not move quickly because the roads were so poor. When the drought occurred on top of these problems, a bad situation became a disaster.

The future

Records of the past climate in Ethiopia show that droughts are a fact of life in this part of the world. The country can expect a major drought at least every 25 years. Yet between 1960 and 1988 there were four periods when the people were in danger of famine. Aid as **famine relief** is only possible in the short term. Long-term help for the farmers and the government are needed to get the country on its feet. Without this the people of Ethiopia can only wait for the next disaster to strike.

▼ *Tens of thousands of people found help in the many refugee camps set up by aid agencies. Here you see people carrying food they have received back to their families who are living in these rows of tents.*

▼ *These children are now recovering their strength thanks to a balanced diet provided by an aid agency.*

Glossary

aid agencies
organizations set up to help people in difficult circumstances by providing food and money for wells and other essentials

anticyclone
a region of downward spiraling air in the atmosphere. It is associated with warming air and does not produce rain.

aqueducts
artifical channels for transporting large amounts of water across the landscape

aquifer
an underground layer of rock and sand that absorbs water and from which water can be withdrawn by wells and pumps

atmosphere
the thick layer of air that surrounds the Earth. It consists of many layers, or shells, each with different properties.

browse
eating bushes and trees (grazing is eating grasses)

climate
the typical pattern of weather at a place. It is normally described by means of temperature, rainfall, etc., averaged over the previous 35 years.

condensation
the change of water vapor to liquid water droplets that occurs when air is cooled. Condensation is often seen on the outside of a glass of cold liquid because air in contact with the glass has been cooled.

conserve water
use water sparingly so that it will last a long time. It also involves using water carefully and to its greatest effect.

continental drought regions
places that suffer drought because they are so far from the oceans and their moisture-bearing winds

deciduous
a plant that loses its leaves seasonally, usually during a dry or a cold season

depression
spiraling regions of the atmosphere where warm and cold air are drawn together. Depressions belong to the midlatitudes and give widespread rain.

desert
a region where rain rarely falls. Deserts have little vegetation and no regular seasonal rain.

developed countries
those countries that have a wide range of industries, and that use most of the world's wealth

developing countries
countries that have not yet fully industrialized and that do not have a wide range of health, water, and other facilities available to the majority of the people. In most developing countries the majority of the people work as farmers.

disaster
a severe event that changes the landscape or disrupts the normal lives of people

drought
a period without rain that is long enough to cause hardship to people, animals, and the plants

epidemic
a disease that spreads quickly and attacks many people in a community

equator
a line around the Earth midway between the poles. The equator marks the center of the region known as the tropics.

erosion
the removal of soil at an unacceptably fast rate. It usually occurs when soil is left bare during a period of heavy rains or strong winds.

evaporation
the loss of water to the air. Evaporated water is held as a gas, not droplets. It is described as "water vapor."

fallow
a period when the land is allowed to rest and is not used for growing crops

famine relief
emergency assistance given to people in danger of starvation

fertile land
land that contains sufficient nutrients to allow crops to grow well

food crops
crops grown especially for food. This consists of most grains, vegetables, and fruits.

Great Depression
a period at the end of the 1920s and early 1930s when many countries in the world had large numbers of people out of work

Green Revolution
the new system of farming introduced to developing countries. It uses scientific methods of growing crops and rearing animals.

high
another name for an anticyclone

irrigation
watering land to allow crops to grow

jet stream
a high-level flow of air that circles the Earth and which "steers" the path of depressions and anticyclones

low
another name for a depression

malnutrition
not getting enough food to remain healthy

monsoon
a name given to the rainy season of the tropics and near tropical lands. It often begins very abruptly.

nomads
people who wander over the landscape with their animals in search of grazing. They have no one settled location.

overuse of land
the growing of crops or grazing of land to such an extent that all the nutrients are used up and the crops and grass can no longer grow properly

pores
small gaps that allow air and water in. Soils need many pores to cope with heavy rainstorms and prevent water from flowing over the surface and causing erosion.

rain shadow zone
the region on the sheltered side of a mountain range that receives low rainfall

reservoir
an artificial lake contained by a dam. It is used to control the amount of water in a river, either to prevent flood or drought.

Sahel
the group of countries lying on the southern margin of Africa's Sahara desert that experience severe drought problems

savanna
a region of tropical grasslands and short trees found where there is a long dry season

soil conservation
methods of reducing the erosion of soil

spring
a source of water coming from the ground sufficient enough to start a stream

starvation
dying from lack of food. Starvation makes the body waste away as it uses up its own reserves of fat and protein (in muscles).

stratosphere
a layer of air in the atmosphere above the troposphere. It does not contain any clouds.

subsidies
paying more for a product than it is really worth in order to help a particular group of people

terraces
platforms or steps made in sloping land to give a flat place for planting seeds. Terraces also prevent soil erosion.

tropics
the part of the Earth nearest to the equator which contains most of the world's hot lands

troposphere
the lowest layer of the atmosphere

water holes
shallow depressions in the land where water is found at the surface

well
a vertical shaft dug into the ground down to the level where water can be found

Index